Gramps Is Not Alone

by Nancy Tyler
illustrated by Len Ebert

Practice Decodable 84

Mc Graw Hill Education

Bothell, WA • Chicago, IL • Columbus, OH • New York, NY

MHEonline.com

Send all inquiries to:
McGraw-Hill Education
8787 Orion Place
Columbus, OH 43240

ISBN: 978-0-02-145428-0
MHID: 0-02-145428-0

Printed in China.

8 9 10 11 12 DSS 27 26 25 24 23

Hope visited Gramps. His house was old. And Gramps was older than his house. He stayed with his dog, Roxie.

Mom and Dad were concerned that Gramps felt lonely. They visited him every week, but Gramps spent much time alone.

"Are you lonely, Gramps?" Hope asked.

Gramps smiled, "Not much. I'm not really alone," he said.

"But you only have Roxie," said Hope.

Gramps smiled, "Let's take a stroll outside. I will show you my pals."

In the yard, Gramps said, "Roxie and I are not alone. Several pals call this place home."

Gramps pointed up.

"See the swallows," said Gramps. "When I wave to the birds, they fly low to say hello."

Hope grinned.

Gramps walked slowly on the stone path. "I do not mow this area so the insects have a home, too."

"Rabbits hide close to this row by the road," Gramps said. "They hop and roam all over."

Gramps stopped by the pond in his yard. "Here, green frogs and toads croak hello to me," he said.

Gramps sat on a swing. He pointed at the house. "See those black bumps below the roof?" he asked.

Hope spotted them. "Those are bats. I let them both stay for free," said Gramps.

Hope's grin grew bigger.

"Can you find the gopher or the skunk?" Gramps asked. "Most days they poke their noses out."

Hope jumped.

"Look closely," said Gramps. Hope stood still and looked closely. She saw birds, squirrels, and a mouse.

"Now you know why I never feel alone," said Gramps.

Hope smiled and gave Gramps a big hug.